HONEST ABE'S FUNNY MONEY BOOK

By Jack Silbert

Scholastic Inc.

New York Toronto London Auckland

Sydney Mexico City New Delhi Hong Kong

To Alexander Hamilton,
who had a bad day
in Weehawken
— J.S.

**Illustrations by
Jim Paillot**

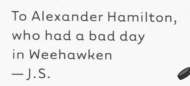

Copyright © 2012 by Scholastic Inc. All rights reserved. Published by Scholastic Inc.
SCHOLASTIC and associated logos are trademarks and/or registered trademarks of
Scholastic Inc.

12 11 10 9 8 7 6 5 4 3 2 1   12 13 14 15 16

ISBN 978-0-545-36740-0

Printed and assembled in China   95

First printing, January 2012

Photo Credits:
All United States coin images courtesy of the United States Mint. Page 14: Native American
Dollar Coin Obverse © 1999 United States Mint. All Rights Reserved. Used with permission.
Pages 16–17: Artist, inspecting coins, metal strip, mold, bag © Bloomberg via Getty Images.
All photos of dollar bills and all photos on pages 28–29 courtesy of the United States Bureau
of Engraving and Printing.

Designed by Janet Kusmierski

CONTENTS

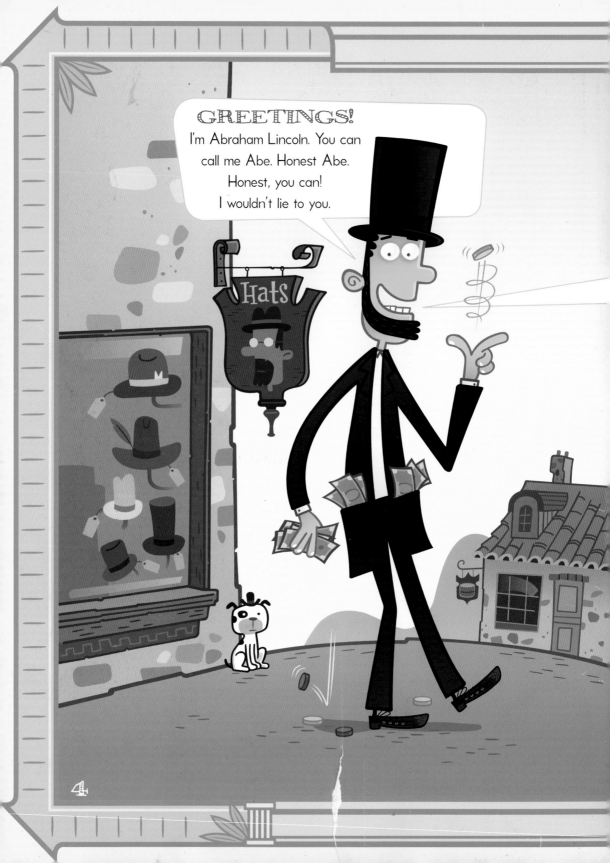

I was the sixteenth President of the United States, from 1861 to 1865. Before that, I was a lawyer and a store clerk. I was known for being really honest, so people called me "Honest Abe."

What am I doing here? I'm here today to talk to you about money. And maybe while I'm around, I'll buy myself a new hat.

Hats cost money. This book cost money. You need money for a lot of things in life. That's why it's important to know about it. What's there to learn about money? Lots!

For starters, have you ever looked at the pictures and words on U.S. coins and paper money and wondered what they mean? I'll tell you all about that. Do you know how our money is made? We'll learn that, too.

Just follow me!

MONEY FROM THEN TO NOW

Money has been around for a long, long time. But it didn't always look like the coins and bills we know today.

Before there was money, people just traded things. Let's say I have food but I need clothes. And you have clothes but need some food. I could trade you some of my food for some of your clothes. Then . . .

11,000 YEARS AGO

People started using animals as money. If you wanted to buy something from someone, you gave that person an animal. Later on, people started using grains and other plants as money.

3,200 YEARS AGO

In China, people started using shells as money. About 200 years later, the Chinese began using metal as money. This money included tools and some of the earliest coins.

YEAR: 806

China came up with another great idea: paper money! The rest of the world didn't catch on for another 800 years or so!

YEAR: 1500

Over here, in the land that would become America, Indians used "wampum" as money. Wampum was a string of beads made from clamshells.

YEARS: 1600s

In the 1600s, early American settlers used money from their former homelands. People used English, Spanish, and French money.

Question:
How did the person with a lot of money introduce himself?

Answer:
Hi, I'm Rich.

2,500 YEARS AGO

In Europe, people started using coins that look somewhat like the ones we use today. They were round and had pictures on them.

1,900 YEARS AGO

Back in China, square pieces of leather were used as money.

YEARS: 1700s

By 1776, the United States of America had become a country. In 1791, the U.S. government set up the First Bank of the United States. The bank began issuing bank notes in dollars and cents. The first American coins were made in 1793.

TODAY

Besides coins and bills, there are many other ways to spend money. You can use checks, credit cards, debit cards, online payments, and more. Still, coins and bills are very important.

Let's learn about all the different coins and bills we use in the United States.

COINS! KA-CHING!

THE PERFECT PENNY

Meet the smallest unit of U.S. currency. The penny is worth one cent. The ¢ symbol stands for cents. One penny is 1¢.

WHAT'S ON THE COIN?
Heads

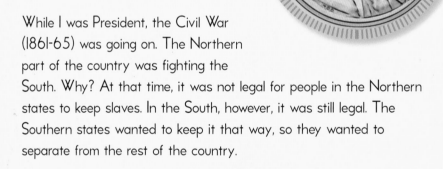

Me! I was born in 1809 in Kentucky. I came from a poor family. But I grew up to be one of the greatest U.S. Presidents ever.

While I was President, the Civil War (1861-65) was going on. The Northern part of the country was fighting the South. Why? At that time, it was not legal for people in the Northern states to keep slaves. In the South, however, it was still legal. The Southern states wanted to keep it that way, so they wanted to separate from the rest of the country.

I helped bring the two sides together again. I also wrote a very famous paper called the Emancipation Proclamation. It led to the end of slavery in America.

Tails

Since 2010, pennies feature this shield. The Latin words mean "Out of many, one."

But what does THAT mean? The original 13 colonies joined together to become the United States of America. So out of many places, we became one big place!

KNOW YOUR DOUGH

▶Look at the coin. Do you see "VDB" below my shoulder? That stands for Victor David Brenner. He designed the heads side of the coin.

▶In 1904, President Theodore Roosevelt wanted U.S. money to have new designs. In 1909, almost 100 years after my birth, I popped up on pennies.

THE NIFTY NICKEL

The nickel is worth 5¢. It's named after one of the metals it is made from.

WHAT'S ON THE COIN?
Heads

Thomas Jefferson was the third U.S. President (1801-1809). He was the main writer of the Declaration of Independence. This famous paper, from 1776, said that we would no longer be controlled by Great Britain. The 13 colonies of Massachusetts, New Hampshire, Connecticut, Rhode Island, New York, New Jersey, Pennsylvania, Maryland, Delaware, Virginia, North Carolina, South Carolina, and Georgia would join together to become the U.S.A.

In 1803, Jefferson helped make the country even bigger. Through the Louisiana Purchase, we bought a giant piece of land from France. That chunk of land now contains all or parts of 15 different U.S. states!

Tails

That's Monticello, Jefferson's home in Virginia. Jefferson designed it himself. Today it is a museum.

THE DANDY DIME

The dime is worth 10¢. It's our smallest and thinnest coin. Its name came from *disme*, an old English word meaning "one-tenth."

WHAT'S ON THE COIN?

Heads

Franklin D. Roosevelt was the thirty-second U.S. President. He served from 1933 to 1945 and helped lead the country out of the Great Depression. This was a tough time in history, starting in 1929, when many people around the world didn't have jobs. Roosevelt started many programs that helped people find work. He also led the U.S. during World War II (1939-45).

Tails

There's a torch, an olive branch, and an oak branch. They stand for liberty, peace, and strength.

KNOW YOUR DOUGH

▶In 1938, President Roosevelt started a charity to fight childhood illnesses. The charity asked everyone in the country to donate one dime to help. The charity became known as the March of Dimes.

▶After President Roosevelt died in 1945, the government honored him by putting him on the dime.

QUITE A QUARTER

The quarter is worth 25¢, or one fourth of a dollar. Another word for one fourth is a quarter.

WHAT'S ON THE COIN?
Heads

Say, "Hi, Dad." That's George Washington, the "Father of Our Country." He was the country's first President (1789–97). He was the only President who was unanimously elected—and twice! Every voter picked him!

Before being President, he was a general. He led America's army during the Revolutionary War (1775–83). During this war, we fought with England. We wanted to win independence from them and become our own nation. Washington's victories helped us do that!

Tails

From 1999 to 2008, the backside of quarters celebrated each of the 50 states. In 2010, we started making quarters that celebrate different national parks.

THE HEAVY HALF DOLLAR

The half dollar is worth 50¢. Maybe you've never seen one before. The half-dollar coin isn't used very often.

WHAT'S ON THE COIN?
Heads

John F. Kennedy was the thirty-fifth U.S. President (1961–63). He created the Peace Corps, a program for young Americans. They go to poor countries and help with teaching, building, and medicine. Kennedy also set a goal to send an American to the moon by the end of the 1960s. Astronaut Neil Armstrong stepped on the moon on July 20, 1969.

Tails

That's the Great Seal of the United States. You'll find this symbol on government documents. The picture has meanings, too. The eagle, our national bird, holds an olive branch and arrows. This represents the power of peace and war. There are 13 arrows and 13 olive leaves. That stands for the original 13 states.

KNOW YOUR DOUGH

▶ The half dollar is the heaviest of all current U.S. coins! It is exactly twice the weight of a quarter.

DELIGHTFUL DOLLAR COINS

The dollar coin is worth 100¢. You know how some people say, "All good things come in pairs"? Guess what? There are TWO different dollar coins!

THE NATIVE AMERICAN DOLLAR COIN
Heads
That's Sacagawea. From 1804 to 1806, she helped explorers Meriwether Lewis and William Clark on a famous expedition.

During that time, America had just expanded with the Louisiana Purchase. But not too many folks from our country had seen what was in that land or beyond. So President Thomas Jefferson sent Lewis and Clark to check it out.

The journey began in Illinois. The duo sailed down the Missouri River. They met Sacagawea in what is now North Dakota. She guided them all the way to the west coast and back.

Tails
Since 2009, this side of the coin features images celebrating the achievements of American Indians.

THE PRESIDENTIAL DOLLAR COIN

Heads

In 2007, we began making special dollar coins to celebrate each of the U.S. Presidents. I was on one in 2010!

Tails

That's the Statue of Liberty. She is one of the best-known symbols of freedom. Lady Liberty was a gift from France. The real statue stands 305 feet tall and overlooks New York Harbor. The statue was completed in 1886.

Question:
How did the George Washington $1 bill feel when he saw the shiny gold Sacagawea coin?

Answer:
He was green with envy.

KNOW YOUR DOUGH

▶ From 1971 to 1978, there was a dollar coin that featured Dwight D. Eisenhower, our thirty-fourth President (1953-61). This coin weighed as much as four quarters!

▶ In 1979, the government came up with a handier coin. Susan B. Anthony, who fought for women's rights, was on the money. It was so similar in size to a quarter, people often mixed them up.

15

WHERE DO COINS COME FROM?

Coins do not fall from the sky. A part of the U.S. government called the U.S. Mint makes all the coins we use. Mint? Like the stuff in green ice cream? No! Mint also means "to make something out of metal."

The U.S. Mint began making coins in 1792 in Philadelphia, Pennsylvania. As the country grew, people needed more coins. Today, besides Philadelphia, there are U.S. Mints in Washington, D.C., New York, Kentucky, Colorado, and California.

The U.S. Mint makes between 65 million and 80 million coins a day. Here's how.

HOW COINS ARE MADE

Artists come up with coin designs.

The blanks go into a "stamping press." This machine is filled with molds of the coin. Bang! The machine stamps pictures on both sides of the blanks.

Officials inspect the coins. Good coins move on to an automatic counting machine. Bad coins get recycled.

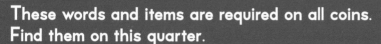
These words and items are required on all coins. Find them on this quarter.

- ☐ United States of America
- ☐ Liberty (or a picture of the Statue of Liberty)
- ☐ In God We Trust
- ☐ E PLURIBUS UNUM
- ☐ The coin's value
- ☐ The year it was made

Machines carve molds containing the pictures that go on the front and back of the coin.

Coins start out as a rolled-up strip of metal. It's about one foot wide and 1,500 feet long! This metal strip feeds into a machine that punches out blank coins.

The coins are bagged and stored in a safe place until banks need them.

Now that you know about every U.S. coin there is today, I think you're ready to learn about paper money. ➡

17

THE DELIGHTFUL DOLLAR BILL

This is the smallest bill we have today. The $ symbol stands for dollars. So we can write that a dollar bill is $1.

WHAT'S ON THE BILL?
Front

That's our old friend George Washington. He first showed up on a dollar bill in 1869. Let's take a closer look.

Seal of the Federal Reserve, the nation's central bank.

Identify which of the 12 Federal Reserve banks issued the note. "B" and "2" stand for New York

Every bill has a unique serial number.

Seal of the U.S. Treasury

The first U.S. dollar bill was made in 1862. It showed a picture of Salmon B. Chase. Who? It's not a guy running after a fish. I knew Chase. During my time in office, he served as the U.S. Secretary of the Treasury (1861-64). He was in charge of all things related to money.

Back

You've seen the great shield before. But why is there a pyramid with a glowing eye on the bill? Pyramids are very strong and last a long time. The bill's designers thought that it's a good way to represent our country. As for the eye? It means there is a power watching over all of us.

Question:
What is a dollar bill's favorite kind of nut?

Answer:
Cash-ew

KNOW YOUR DOUGH

▶Back in the 1800s, paper money was huge. Each bill measured more than 7 inches long and over 3 inches wide. In 1929, all our paper money became the size it still is today—6.14 inches long by 2.61 inches wide.

▶Think the dollar bill is small? The smallest we ever produced was a three-cent bill printed in 1865!

THE TERRIFIC TWO-DOLLAR BILL!

Have you ever seen a $2 bill? No? It's real money. I promise!

WHAT'S ON THE BILL?
Front

Remember Thomas Jefferson? Besides being the country's third President, he was our second-ever Vice President. He served under John Adams (1797–1801). He was also the nation's first Secretary of State, working for George Washington (1789-93). But that's not all! He also founded the University of Virginia.

Back

These are members of the Continental Congress. They represented each of the 13 colonies. They got together and wrote the Declaration of Independence in 1776. You'll find Jefferson here.

STOPPING PHONY MONEY

You might not believe the $2 bill is real money, but it is. However, there are crooks who purposely try to make fake money. This is called counterfeiting.

The U.S. government has tried many ways to fight counterfeiting. Check out some security features they've hidden into bills in the amounts of $5 and up. These features are hard for crooks to duplicate:

Security Thread

Hold the bill up to the light again. See a thin strip that goes from the top of the bill to the bottom. Its line is made of "USA" and the bill's worth in supertiny letters!

Watermarks

Hold the front of a bill up to the light. Do you see a faint image popping up like a ghost?

Color-Shifting Ink

On $10, $20, $50, and $100 bills, look at the bill's amount in the lower-right front corner. Tilt the bill. The number changes from copper to green.

THE FABULOUS FIVE-DOLLAR BILL

Who is that handsome man on the $5 bill? Honest Abe!

WHAT'S ON THE BILL?

Front

I first appeared on a $5 bill in 1914. My picture used to be about the same size as George's on the $1 bill. In 2000, the government put new pictures on money. So I wound up with a bigger head.

Back

That's the Lincoln Memorial in Washington, D.C., our nation's capital. It celebrates me! There are 36 columns. They represent the number of states we had when I was President. Carved on the memorial are the names of 48 states. We had that many when the building was finished in 1922. Alaska and Hawaii joined the nation in 1959.

FUN ABE FACTS

On the pages about the penny, you learned some important facts about me. Now, let me tell you about some fun stuff!

I shot a turkey at age seven. But you know what? Doing this made me really, really sad. I didn't like hunting after that.

I have more than one nickname. I am also called "Rail Splitter." That's because when I was a young man, I chopped wood. We had to split logs to make the rails for fences.

I like animals. My son Tad kept two pet goats at the White House!

I still am the tallest U.S. President ever. I am six feet four inches tall—that's without my hat!

I ♥ gingerbread cookies. My mom used to make them for me.

Question:
What did Mama and Papa Dollar name their baby son?

Answer:
Bill

23

THE TERRIFIC TEN-DOLLAR BILL

See the guy on the $10 bill? He's the only person on all U.S. paper money to look to the left.

WHAT'S ON THE BILL?

Front

That's Alexander Hamilton. He is the only person on U.S. money who wasn't born here! He was born in the Caribbean.

Remember Salmon B. Chase? The guy who was on the $1 bill, right before George took over? Hamilton had the same job from 1789 to 1795. In fact, he was the very first U.S. Secretary of the Treasury. He set up a real banking system for the country.

Back

That's the Treasury Building in Washington, D.C. It's the headquarters of the U.S. Treasury Department. See the statue in front of the building? It's of Alexander Hamilton!

KNOW YOUR DOUGH:

▶ Hamilton is one of only two non-Presidents who currently appear on U.S. paper money. You'll meet the other one soon.

THE EQUALLY TERRIFIC TWENTY-DOLLAR BILL

The guy on the $20 bill might not be happy to find his face there. Why? He didn't like paper money. He preferred coins.

WHAT'S ON THE BILL?

Front

Andrew Jackson was the seventh U.S. President, from 1829 to 1837. He served for two terms. During that time, Arkansas and Michigan joined the United States. Jackson was tough, so his nickname was "Old Hickory." (That's a type of wood.)

His first inauguration—the ceremony to become President—is also famous. It was the first one opened to the public.

Back

It's the White House in Washington, D.C. Every President has lived there except George Washington. The White House was just being built when he was President.

Question:
Why did the guest give money to his host?

Answer:
He was paying a visit.

THE FANTASTIC FIFTY-DOLLAR BILL

The $50 bill is worth 200 quarters. That's too many coins to carry.

WHAT'S ON THE BILL?
Front
Ulysses S. Grant was the eighteenth U.S. President. He was in office from 1869 to 1877. Before that, he was commander of the Union Army (from the North) in the Civil War. He was President during Reconstruction. During this time, new state governments were set up in the South. Also, laws were passed to give better treatment to former slaves.

Back
It's a picture of the U.S. Capitol building. That's where the Congress meets in Washington, D.C. Congress is the group of people from all over the country who make our laws.

KNOW YOUR DOUGH

▶There used to be $500, $1,000, $5,000, and $10,000 bills. The government stopped printing them in 1945.

THE HISTORIC HUNDRED-DOLLAR BILL

The $100 bill is the largest amount you'll find in U.S. paper money.

WHAT IS ON THE BILL?

Front

Earlier on I said there are two non-Presidents on U.S. paper money. Meet Benjamin Franklin.

Franklin wore many hats. He was a printer and a writer known for his humor and wisdom. He was also a scientist and inventor of such things as bifocal glasses and swim flippers! Franklin also started a library and a fire station. He was the first person in charge of the U.S. Post Office!

Back

That's Independence Hall in Philadelphia, Pennsylvania. The signing of the Declaration of Independence took place here. Back then, the building was known as the Pennsylvania State House. The clock on top of the building shows 4:10.

Question:
What do you call money that screams a lot?

Answer:
Hundred-holler bill.

WHERE DO BILLS COME FROM?

Our paper money does not grow on trees. If they did, I'd be racking it in. U.S. paper money is made by the Bureau of Engraving and Printing (BEP). This government department has been printing bills since 1877.

The BEP has two locations. There is one in Washington, D.C., and one in Texas. In 2010, the BEP printed 26 million bills each day. The total value of the bills printed every day was worth about $974 million dollars.

HOW BILLS ARE MADE

Artists create the design of the bill.

The design is then carved on large printing plates. The printing plate goes into a machine that will print the money.

Inspectors study the big sheets. The good ones are split in half, into two 16-bill sheets.

Then more numbers and seals are printed on the smaller sheets. A special computer inspects these sheets again.

A machine cuts the good she into separate bills. A paper be goes around 100 bills of the s amount (100 one-dollar bills, example).

KNOW YOUR DOUGH

▶Paper money is pretty sturdy. You could fold it about 4,000 times before it would rip. But don't try it! It is against the law to damage money on purpose.

What happens when money gets too old and worn out to handle? People can exchange them for new bills at any local bank. Banks send the old money to the Federal Reserve Bank, the nation's central bank. The worn-out money is destroyed.

Money starts as big sheets of paper. You can fit 32 bills on it. This paper is made of cotton and linen.

The paper goes into the printing machine. It prints the words and pictures on the money one side at a time.

The government stores the bills in a safe place. They ship fresh bills to banks whenever they are needed.

SMART MONEY

You now know a lot about money. But how do you get money?
You have to work for it.

RAKE IT IN

What's one way for kids to make money? You can start a lemonade stand!
How much you earn depends on how many glasses you sell. Let's say you
charge $0.10 for a glass. You sell 20 glasses. This is how you find your
earnings: $ 0.10 x 20 = $2.00.

Finish the chart below to see how I did running a lemonade stand.

Honest Abe's Lemonade Stand

Day	Cost per glass	Glasses sold	Sales
7/1	$0.10	50	$5.00
7/2	$0.10	70	$7.00
7/3	$0.10	80	
7/4	$0.10	70	
TOTAL SALES (ADD UP YOUR DAILY SALES):			
COST OF SUPPLIES (LEMONS, SUGAR, CUPS):			-$7.00
HONEST ABE'S TOTAL EARNINGS:			

Turn this book upside down to find Honest Abe's Total Earnings.

What's this? It costs money to set up a business.
Subtract the amount spent from the Total Sales.

KEEP YOUR BALANCE

You've got some money to spend. But it is no fun if you spend more money than you have. You go into a situation called debt. That means you owe people money. What's the best way to avoid debt? Keep track of how much money you have. This is also called your balance. Keeping a balance is easy. Just make a table like the one below.

Question:
What kind of pants do coins like to wear?

Answer:
Quarter-oy

Abe's Piggy Bank Balance

Date	Saving/Spending	Amount	Balance
4/1	Gift from Grandma	$20	$20
4/2	Bought a comic book	-$3	$17
4/5	Dog-sitting $5 x 2 hours	$10	

Turn this book upside down to find Abe's balance.

#1 Every time you save or spend money, write it down here.

#2 Record the amount you saved or spent here.

#3 When you saved money, add the amount you saved here. When you spent, subtract the amount you used. Find the balance in your piggy bank.

Answers: Honest Abe's Total Earnings $20
Abe's Piggy Bank Balance $27

FUNNY MONEY

Question:
What do you say when you understand how money works?

Answer:
That makes cents.

FINAL WORDS FROM HONEST ABE

You are now a master of money! It's time for me to go back to the 1860s. I was going to buy a new hat while I was here, but I think I'll keep the one I have. It still looks pretty good, don't you think?

If you want to learn even more about money, the U.S. government has many fun Web sites just for kids! You can find them all at **www.usmint.gov/kids**

If you ever miss me, you can always find me on a penny or a five-dollar bill. One thing you know about Honest Abe: I'm always on the money!